BEGINNING STORIES
FROM THE HEART

Ronna Magy

Linda Mrowicki, Editor

Photography by:
Daniel Jackson
Pauline Thom

Cover design by:
Sally Richardson

LINMORE PUBLISHING Box 1545 Palatine, IL 60078 (800) 336-3656

Linmore Publishing
PO Box 1545
Palatine, IL 60078
(800) 336-3656

ⓒ   Linmore Publishing, Inc. 1995

First Printing, 1995
Printed in the United States of America

BEGINNING STORIES FROM THE HEART
ISBN   0-916591 32-8

Acknowledgements:

Thanks to the following teachers for their participation in this project: **Inez Aidlin, Angela Locke, Mim Paggi,** and **Barbara Hughes** at South Gate Adult Learning Center; **Lynn Suio** at Gardena Adult School; **Valerie Estes** at Abram Friedman Occupational Center; **Elaine Klapman** at Venice Adult Learning Center; **Pauline Thom** at Los Angeles High School; **Patricia Tkach** at Evans Adult School; **Ronette Youmans** at Fairfax High School, and **Beth Easter** and **Jane Sevald** at the Adult Literacy Program of the Minneapolis Public Schools.

A special thank you to all the student writers who allowed their stories to be told in this volume so that other students could talk about and write their own personal stories.

Special thanks to **Steve Barba**, Principal, and **Joanne Abing**, Assistant Principal, South Gate Adult School; **Steve Austin**, Bilingual Coordinator, Los Angeles High School, **Mayra Fernandez**, and **Beth Lishner** for their ongoing support in this project.

Photo Credits:
The following people kindly allowed themselves to be photographed:
Andrew Cetwinski, Brad Goode, Mary & Tom Jackson, Douglas Jones, Pauline Thom, Vera and Willard Beebe

Dedication:
This book is dedicated to **Gert Levine** and **Bess Carp**, two loving aunts, who have been with me throughout this writing process and all my life, and to **Frances Eisenberg**, my mentor teacher.

TEACHER'S INTRODUCTION

Beginning Stories From the Heart is a reading and writing book for secondary and adult students who are at the high beginning stage of language acquisition. The text consists of six units: About Me, School, Favorite Things, Special Events, First Country/Second Country, and Decisions. Each unit contains authentic student stories - stories written by students from their own life experiences. From describing the neighbor next door to taking a test, from Chinese and Ethiopian New Year celebrations to a mother's conflict over going to an ESL class or taking care of her daughter, the stories are poignant, lively, and compelling. Within each lesson, students are taken on a journey through the lives of others that leads them to their own story writing. All the stories in **Beginning Stories From The Heart** are written by high school and adult students. Editing of the stories has been limited to correction of those mistakes which would affect the ability of the reader to comprehend the writer's message. The stories reflect the writers' experiences while modeling good reading and writing practice.

Using a whole language approach, each lesson consists of activities and student stories linked to a lesson theme. The theme is developed through pre-reading activities, an authentic student story, a comprehension check, and follow-up writing. Speaking, listening, and reading activities build so that individual students may draw on their own and life experiences in writing sentences and then, a paragraph about themselves. Cooperative learning activities incorporating whole class, small group, pair, and individual practice are woven into each lesson.

Each units concludes with a Think About the Unit section allowing students to reflect on the unit's stories as well as on their own writing, a Find Someone activity and a guided image based on the lesson theme.

Beginning Stories from the Heart incorporates current learning theory and practice in its approach. The text adheres to a whole language philosophy by relating the book content to a student's own experiences and beliefs. All four language areas - listening, speaking, reading, and writing are carefully integrated in the materials. Cooperative leaning activities are built into the lessons to allow the sharing of information and experiences, peer teaching/learning, practice in a variety of group processes, and the opportunity to acquire language in a meaningful context. The text encourages students to share their stories with a partner and give positive feedback. Thus, at this stage, students begin the writing process with peer as well as teacher feedback.

CONTENTS

Each unit begins with an activity which focuses students' attention on the stories and the countries the student authors come from. The unit concludes with activities which provide the students with the opportunity to interact with each other and to reflect on their impressions of the unit.

Each lesson contains three sections: Pre-Reading, Reading of an Authentic Story and Post Reading, and Writing. Specific activities for each section include:

Pre-reading Cooperative Activities	Reading & Post Reading Activities	Writing Activities
Brainstorm.	Silent and Oral Reading.	Pre-writing.
Look at the Photo/Picture.	Check Your Understanding.	Writing.
Draw a picture.	Pair Reading.	Sharing and feedback.
Picture Re-tell.		
Group Survey.		
Take a Turn.		
Line-Up.		
Corners.		
Stand Up and Share.		
Give Your Opinion.		

HOW TO USE THIS BOOK

The following are suggestions on how to use the book. Teachers should feel free to adapt the material in this book to their own teaching styles and to each class of students.

BEGINNING OF UNIT:

The first page of each unit introduces the story titles, the names of the authors, and the countries they are from. A map gives students the opportunity to identify the geographical location of the countries.

LESSON:

Each lesson introduces a theme-related issue for students to discuss with their classmates. These oral-aural activities lead to story reading, further discussion, and sentence and paragraph writing. Recommended steps for using the lessons are:

Pre-Reading/Cooperative Activities:

These activities are for whole class, small group, and pair work. An activity may be a discussion, a line-up, a brainstorm, or a charting exercise. Whatever the activity, the participation of all students is essential. Following some of the activities, the individual's and/or small group's information is shared with the whole class orally or on the chalkboard. Specific steps for the activities are:

Look at the Photo/Picture: Students look at the introductory lesson visual and discuss guided questions about the lesson theme.

Brainstorm With Your Class / In a Small Group: In the class brainstorm, the teacher introduces the lesson theme and asks the class to call out any words that come to mind. For example: *"Today we're going to talk about your neighborhood. When you think of your neighborhood, what do you think about? The streets? The buildings? The cars?"* All words called out by the students are recorded on the chalkboard by the teacher and in their books by the students.

In the small group brainstorm, students sit in a group of three or four. The teacher introduces the lesson theme to the class. Each student in the group suggests words for the group list. Each student writes all the words in his or her own book. Group recorders share their group's list with the class orally or on the chalkboard. The teacher points out similarities and differences between the groups' lists. The activity is limited to 5 - 10 minutes.

Draw a Picture: Individual students draw a picture of a person or some other aspect of the lesson theme. After drawing the picture, students participate either in a follow-up sharing activity with another student or a brief individual written exercise.

Picture-Retell: Students sit with a partner and talk about a picture(s) using a guided question format.

Group Survey: Students sit in a group of three or four. Students' names are listed in the first column of the chart. The group elects a leader who asks each student the written questions. All students record everyone's responses. Following the chart, a series of questions helps each group to analyze and summarize their information.

Take a Turn: Students sit in a group of four or with a partner. Each has two minutes to give an opinion or answer a question.

Line-Up: Students form a line based on their responses to a question. For example, if the question is, *"When is your birthday?"*, the line is formed based on the chronology of the students' birthdays. After students line up, the teacher checks by asking the question back to most students in the line. This activity may be followed by a pair discussion between members of the line.

Corners: Students go to one of the four corners of the room as designated by the teacher. For example, *"If you are wearing blue jeans, please go to Corner 1."* In the corner, students talk to a partner about a related subject.

Stand Up and Share: All students in the class stand up. The teacher introduces a topic, such as the thing you liked best about your country. The teacher calls on one student to answer. For example, a student may say, *"I like the food."* The teacher thanks the student and asks the students to sit down. Then, all the other students who selected food as their first choice also sit down. Then the teacher calls on another student. The second student and the students who agree sit down. The activity continues until all students are seated.

Give Your Opinion: Working individually, students express their opinion in an agree/disagree activity and then share their opinions with another student.

READING THE STORY:

1. The teacher introduces the story by focusing students' attention on the bottom of the first lesson page: *"Let's read a story about ..."*.

2. The teacher introduces the story title and the photo and asks students to predict what the story will be about.

3. The teacher summarizes the students' predictions. At this time, the teacher may choose to introduce any key vocabulary which she or he feels may be new to the class.

4. The students read the story silently.

5. The teacher asks students for comments on the story contents, their reactions, or any questions they may have.

6. The teacher reads the story orally while students read along silently.

7. The students read the story aloud in pairs.

POST-READING:

Check Your Understanding: This is an oral and written activity which focuses on the author's main idea or intent and then on comprehension of important story details. Suggested steps are:

1. Students talk about the questions with the class.

2. Students individually answer the questions.

3. The teacher checks the accuracy of the answers by reviewing individual responses, checking the answers with the class, and using cooperative checking.

Write A Story: This section focuses on the students' writing their own personal stories. Suggested steps are:

1. Students talk about the questions with a partner.

2. Students write the answers to the questions.

3. Students use their answers to write a paragraph.

4. Students share their stories with a partner and supportive feedback is given by the partner.

Three suggested follow-up activities to use with the students' personal stories are:

Group - Share: Students sit in a group of three or four and read their stories aloud. The other students in the group listen closely. When the reading is finished, each listener asks one question about the story.

Art Gallery: The teacher checks individual student writing for major errors such as incorrect verb tenses or spelling. Students then recopy their stories. The stories are posted art gallery style around the classroom. As members of the class read each story, they are asked to note the name of the writer and something they liked about each story. Then students sit in small groups and discuss which story was the most interesting, the funniest, and the most serious, and why.

Cross Class Share: Another class is invited in and the student writers share their stories.

END OF UNIT ACTIVITIES:

Find Someone: This is an interactive activity for the whole class. The exercise consists of a list of blank lines with answers such as, *"1. _____ lives in a house."* Before beginning the activity, the teacher helps the students to form questions for each statement, such as, *"Do you live in a house?"* After this initial practice, the steps are:
   1. Students circulate around the class and ask other students the questions.
   2. If a student gives an affirmative answer, the student is asked to sign her or his name on the correct line.

Guided Image: This is a valuable activity for triggering students' thoughts and memories and focusing them on a topic. Students relax, close their eyes, and make a picture in their minds as they listen to the teacher slowly reading the guided image script. (These scripts are found on page v.) In the written script, each series of dots (...) represents a five second pause in voice time, allowing the students' minds to focus on the images as they develop. When the image is completed, the students slowly open their eyes and talk about what they saw, felt, and experienced. The teacher asks questions such as, "What did you see?" How did you feel?" Then, students write about what they experienced.

A suggested relaxing exercise is: *"Breathe in slowly ... Breathe out slowly ... Breathe in slowly ... Breathe out slowly ... Sit comfortably in your chair ... Close your eyes ... Relax your head ... your neck ... your back ... your legs ... Breathe in and out slowly ... Listen to my voice ... Make a picture in your mind from the words ... Breathe in slowly ... Breathe out slowly."*

Think About The Unit: This is a reflective exercise in which students select their favorite story from the book, choose their own favorite personal story, and briefly describe the reasons for their selections. Their responses are then shared with a partner.

TEACHER'S GUIDED IMAGE SCRIPTS

About Me - Guided Image:

Close your eyes ... Breathe in and out slowly ... In your mind, make a picture of your neighborhood ... Think about your street ... the trees ... the cars ... the buildings ... Think about your home ... your family or roommates ... your neighbors ... your friends ... the adults ... the children playing ... Think about something you like about your neighborhood ... Breathe in and out slowly ... Open your eyes.

School - Guided Image:

Close your eyes ... Breathe in and out slowly ... In your mind, make a picture of your school ... the building ... this classroom ... the teacher... your friends ... our lessons ... Think about what you are studying and learning here ... Think of a class you really like ... Think of something to do with friends after school ... Smile ... Breathe in and out slowly ... Open your eyes.

Favorite Things - Guided Image:

Close your eyes ... Breathe in and out slowly ... In your mind, think of dancing your favorite dance ... Listen to the music ... Move your body to the music ... Dance around the room ... Feel the music in your arms and legs ... Smile at your friends ... Enjoy the music ... Remember the dance ... Breathe in and out slowly ... Open your eyes.

Special Event - Guided Image:

Close your eyes ... Breathe in and out slowly ... In your mind, make a picture of a special day you like to celebrate ... a holiday ... a birthday ... Imagine you are there ... Look around the room ... Listen to the music ... Talk to the people you know ... Eat the wonderful food ... listen to the music ... You feel excited and happy ... Smile ... Slowly come back to the classroom ... Open your eyes.

First Country/Second Country - Guided Image:

Close your eyes ... Breathe in and out slowly ... In your mind, make a picture of your country ... the land ... the weather ... the people ... the holidays ... the special food ... the clothing. Think of some things you like there .. Now, think about the United States and this city ... the land ... the weather ... the people .. the holidays ... the food ... What is different about this country?... What do you like about it? ... Slowly come back to the room ... Open your eyes.

Decisions - Guided Image:

Close your eyes ... Breathe in and out slowly ... Make a picture in your mind of a beautiful place you like to go to ... Imagine you are relaxing in that beautiful place ... under a tree ... or in the sun ... You are thinking about a problem ... What is the problem? ... Think about explaining your problem to an old friend ... Talk to your friend about the problem ... Listen to your friend's advice ... Think about what you can do ... Open your eyes.

Beginning Stories from the Heart

CONTENTS

ABOUT ME 1

Lesson 1:   **About My Family** 2
    "My Family" by Chai Lor, Laos... 3

Lesson 2:   **About My Street** 5
    "My Street" by Caroline Pradel Yuling, Haiti 6

Lesson 3:   **About My Neighborhood** 8
    " My Neighborhood" by Yeon-Jin (Jina) Heoh, South Korea 9

Lesson 4:   **About My Neighbors** 11
    "About My Neighbors" by Chong Won Chon, South Korea 12
    "My Nasty Neighbor" by Adriana Baltazar, Mexico 12

SCHOOL 15

Lesson 5:   **Enrolling in School** 16
    "My First Day" by Zoila Chagoya, Mexico 17

Lesson 6:   **My School** 19
    "My School" by Luisa Ochoa, Honduras 20

Lesson 7:   **My Best Friend** 22
    "My Best Friend" by Cesar Gutierrez, Mexico 23

Lesson 8:   **Homework** 25
    "My Homework" by Vadik Mendelson, Russia 26

Lesson 9:   **Tests** 28
    "The Test" by Yelena Tovbina, Ukraine 29

Lesson 10:   **After-School Activities** 31
    "My Favorite Sport - Gymnastics" by Georgina Serrano, Mexico........... 32
    "Volleyball" by Maria de Jesus Hernandez, Mexico 32

FAVORITE THINGS 35

Lesson 11:   **Favorite Food** 36
    "Stuffed Chicken" by Fidelia Cadenas, Nicaragua 37

Lesson 12:   **Favorite Clothes** 39
    "Sandals" by Mario Castellanos, Mexico 40

Lesson 13:   **Favorite Activity** 42
    "Dancing" by Jose Cardozo, Mexico 43

SPECIAL EVENTS..47

Lesson 14: **New Year's Day** 48
  "Chinese New Year" by Cindy Tse, China 49
  "Ethiopian New Year" by Mulugeta Gebrmichael, Ethiopia 50

Lesson 15: **An Important Birthday** 52
  "Quinceañera" by Trinidad Nuñez, Mexico 53

Lesson 16: **Independence Day** 55
  "Honduran Independence Day" by Marco Martinez, Honduras 56

Lesson 17: **Mother's Day or Father's Day** 58
  "Mother's Day" by Flor Galindo, Mexico 59

FIRST COUNTRY / SECOND COUNTRY 63

Lesson 18: **Life in My Country** 64
  "Life in Cuba" by Luis Felipe Morgan, Cuba 65

Lesson 19: **Deciding to Leave My Country** 67
  "Deciding to Leave El Salvador" by Norma Irene Mendoza, El Salvador 68

Lesson 20: **My Trip to the United States**..70
  "Coming to the U.S." by Nada Chambers, Yugoslavia 71

Lesson 21: **First Impressions of the United States** 73
  "My First Day in the U.S." by My Duyen Thi Nguyen, Vietnam 74

DECISIONS 77

Lesson 22: **Family Rules** 78
  "The Car" by Gennady Daych, Russia 79

Lesson 23: **Losing Someone** 81
  "Death of My Friend" by Hyung Min Jeon, South Korea........................82

Lesson 24: **Getting Advice** 84
  "My Father's Advice" by Young J. Lee, South Korea 85

Lesson 25: **A Family Problem** 87
  "When My Brother Ran Away" by Hwa Jin Oh, South Korea 88

Lesson 26: **A Problem** 90
  "My Problem" by Martina Banda, Mexico 91

ABOUT ME

INTRODUCTION TO THE UNIT.

This unit has stories from five students. These are the stories:

My Family by Chai Lor, Laos

My Street by Caroline Pradel Yuling, Haiti

My Neighborhood by Yeon-Jin (Jina) Heoh, South Korea

About My Neighbors by Chong Won Chon, South Korea

My Nasty Neighbor by Adriana Baltazar, Mexico

The students come from four countries - Laos, Haiti, Korea, and Mexico.

Can you draw their countries on the map?

1: ABOUT MY FAMILY

BRAINSTORM WITH YOUR CLASS: Think about your family and make a list of family members.

Examples: mother, father, grandmother

_____ _____ _____

_____ _____ _____

_____ _____ _____

_____ _____ _____

DRAW A PICTURE OF YOU AND YOUR FAMILY.

Show your picture to a partner. Talk about you and your family. Answer these questions.

1. What's your name?
2. Where is your family from?
3. How many people are in your family?
4. Who is in your family?
5. What are their names?

Let's read a student's story about his family.

My Family
by **Chai Lor**
Adult Literacy Program of Minneapolis Public Schools

    My name is Chai. There are five people in my family. My wife's name is Lor. I have three children. My daughters' names are Pa, Mai, and Hlee. My children are six, four, and two years old. I have one sister. Her name is Plia. She is twenty years old. She lives in Laos. I live in Minneapolis.

Share with a partner: What do you like about Chai's story?

CHECK YOUR UNDERSTANDING: Talk about these questions with your class. Then write your answers.

1. Who is in Chai's family? _____

2. What is his wife's name? _____

3. What are his children's names? _____

4. Where does he live? _____

5. Where does his sister live? _____

WRITE A STORY: Talk about these questions with a partner. Then write your answers.

1. What is your name? _____

2. What are the names of the people in your family? _____

_____

3. How old are they? _____

_____

4. Where do they live? _____

Write a story about you and your family.

My Family

_____

_____

_____

_____

_____

_____

Read your story to a partner.
Then your partner can share something she or he liked about your story.

2: ABOUT MY STREET

BRAINSTORM WITH YOUR CLASS: Think about your street and make a list of words.
Examples: buildings, cars, quiet

_____   _____   _____

_____   _____   _____

_____   _____   _____

_____   _____   _____

DRAW A PICTURE OF YOUR STREET: Include buildings, trees, cars, and other things.

Read the sentences. Circle True or False. Then check your answers with the class.

1. My street is quiet.	True	False
2. My street is dangerous.	True	False
3. Many cars park on my street.	True	False
4. Buses drive on my street.	True	False
5. An ice cream truck drives on my street.	True	False
6. Children play on my street.	True	False
7. Neighbors sit outside and talk.	True	False

Let's read a student's story about her street.

My Street
by Caroline Pradel Yuling

Los Angeles High School

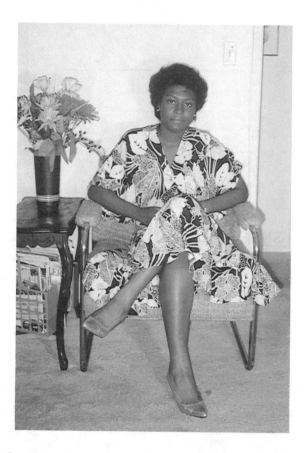

I live with my parents, my sister, and brothers. My apartment is on the second floor. My neighbors are very friendly. They are from all the countries, Korea, China, Japan, Mexico, Nigeria, and France. Some are from Los Angeles.

I live on a quiet street. The only noise you can hear is at 4:00 when the ice cream truck is passing. You can go out at any time you want. The street has two little houses and many buildings. It is near a market and a laundry.

Share with a partner: What do you like about Caroline's story?

CHECK YOUR UNDERSTANDING: Talk about these questions with your class. Then write your answers.

1. Does Caroline live in a house or an apartment? _____

2. Is her street quiet or noisy? _____

3. Which other buildings are on her street?_____

_____

WRITE A STORY: Talk about these questions with a partner. Then write your answers.

1. Do you live in an apartment or a house? _____

2. What street do you live on? _____

3. Is your street busy or noisy? _____

4. How many houses or apartment buildings are on your street? _____

_____

5. What other buildings are on your street? _____

_____

Write a story about your street.

About My Street

_____

_____

_____

_____

_____

_____

Read your story to a partner.
Then your partner can share something he or she liked about your story.

3: ABOUT MY NEIGHBORHOOD

LOOK AT THE PHOTO: Discuss the questions with your class.

1. What is a neighborhood?
2. Who lives next door to you?
3. Do you talk to your neighbors?
   In what language?

GROUP SURVEY: Work in a group of four. Write the names of the students in your group. Ask the questions below and fill in the chart.

Do you live in a house or an apartment?

How many people do you live with?

Do you like your neighbors?

Name	House	Ap't.	No. of people	Likes neighbors	Doesn't like neighbors
Example: *Karla*		X	4	X	

Answer the questions about your group's chart.

1. How many students in your group live in a house? _____
2. How many students live in an apartment? _____
3. How many students live alone? _____
4. How many students like their neighbors? _____

Let's read a student's story about her neighborhood.

My Neighborhood
by Yeon-Jin (Jina) Heoh
Los Angeles High School

I have a very nice neighborhood. There is a house next door. It has a pretty garden. Two families live in the house. One lives on the first floor, and the other lives on the second floor. It's a very pretty house with a little garden. A young woman who is the owner lives on the second floor. She is single. She leaves home early and gets home late.

On the first floor, there is a young husband and wife. One night when I was opening my window, I saw a candle in their window. After a few seconds, I saw that the couple was dancing. It was very lovely for me. They looked very happy at that moment. I hope they will be in love forever.

I love my neighborhood. I can see many things.

Share with a partner: What do you like about Jina's story?

CHECK YOUR UNDERSTANDING: Talk about these questions with your class. Then write your answers.

1. How many families live in the house next to Jina's house? _____

_____

2. Who lives on the first floor? _____

3. Who lives on the second floor? _____

4. What did Jina see out her window? _____

_____

WRITE A STORY: Talk about these questions with a partner. Then write your answers.

1. Who lives next door to you? _____

2. Who do you see when you look out the window? _____

_____

3. What do you see when you look out the window? _____

_____

Write a story about your neighborhood.

About My Neighborhood

_____

_____

_____

_____

_____

_____

Read your story to a partner.
Then your partner can share something she or he liked about your story.

4: ABOUT MY NEIGHBORS

LOOK AT THE PHOTO: Discuss the questions with your class.

1. Do you have any neighbors who make a lot of noise?

2. Do you have any neighbors who have a barking dog?

3. Do you have any neighbors who fight?

4. Do you have any neighbors who give you food?

5. Do you have any neighbors who go to the store for you?

6. Do you have any neighbors who watch your home when you are away?

7. What does a good neighbor do?

8. What does a bad neighbor do?

TAKE A TURN IN A GROUP OF FOUR: Each person has two minutes to talk.

What are some things you like about your neighbors?

What are some things you don't like about your neighbors?

Begin your answer with: My neighbors are _____

because _____

_____

Let's read two students' stories about their neighbors.

About My Neighbors

by Chong Won Chon

Los Angeles High School

I live in an apartment. It has two bedrooms. I like this apartment. I like to live in this building. My neighbors are very kind. Maybe fifty families live in this building.

I live in room 306. A man lives on the left side of me. He's from Bangladesh. He lives alone. He is a nurse. Every day I can smell his country's food. The smell is good. One day he gave me some cake. So, my father gave him some Korean food.

My apartment manager is a good neighbor. His family helped my family a lot. They are very kind. You can see I like my neighbors.

My Nasty Neighbor

by Adriana Baltazar

Los Angeles High School

Two houses from my house lives an old and angry man. He always complains about the other neighbors. On our corner on weekends, a lot of people come to sell food. This man is always looking for what is wrong. He scares the other people. He tells them that they cannot sell food on the corner. He says that what they are doing is not allowed by law. He is bitter. I think he is rich, but he is poor in feelings. He doesn't care what these people have to risk selling food without permission. Sometimes he calls the police. When the police come, they give the people a ticket.

I think this man wanted to be a politician, but he didn't win. That is why he is always complaining.

SHARE WITH A PARTNER: What do you like about their stories?

CHECK YOUR UNDERSTANDING: Read the questions and put an X in the correct column. Then check your answers with the class.

	Chong Won	Adriana
1. Who lives in an apartment?	X	
2. Who lives in a house?		X
3. Who likes their neighbors?	X	
4. Who doesn't like their neighbors?		X
5. Whose neighbor is from Bangladesh?	X	
6. Whose neighbor calls the police?		X
7. Whose neighbor is old and rich?		X
8. Whose neighbor cooks special food?	X	

WRITE A STORY: Talk about these questions with a partner. Then write your answers.

1. What is your neighbor's name? _____

2. Where does your neighbor live? _____

3. When do you see your neighbor? _____

4. What do you talk to your neighbor about? _____

Write a story about one of your neighbors.

About My Neighbor

_____

_____

_____

_____

_____

_____

Read your story to a partner.
Then your partner can share something he or she liked about your story.

Beginning Stories from the Heart

FIND SOMEONE*: Ask your classmates a question. If your classmate's answer is "Yes," ask your classmate to write his or her name on the line next to the sentence.

1. _____ has a friendly neighbor.

2. _____ has a noisy neighbor.

3. _____ lives near a park.

4. _____ lives in a quiet neighborhood.

5. _____ has neighbors from the U.S.

6. _____ speaks English with the neighbors.

GUIDED IMAGE*: Close your eyes and think about your neighborhood. Now begin to write.

When I closed my eyes:

1. I saw _____

2. I heard _____

3. I smelled _____

4. I felt _____

THINK ABOUT THE UNIT: Answer the questions. Discuss your answers with a partner.

1. Circle the lesson you think is the most interesting: 1   2   3   4

   Why do you like it? _____

2. Circle the student's story you like the most: **My Family**   **My Street**
   My Neighborhood   **My Neighbors** (Chong Won)   **My Nasty Neighbor** (Adriana)
   Why do you like it? _____

3. Write the title of your story that you like the best. _____

   Why do you like it? _____

SCHOOL

INTRODUCTION TO THE UNIT.

This unit has stories from seven students. These are the stories:

My First Day by Zoila Chagoya, Mexico

My School by Luisa Ochoa, Honduras

My Best Friend by Cesar Gutierrez, Mexico

My Homework by Vadik Mendelson, Russia

The Test by Yelena Tovbina, Ukraine

My Favorite Sports - Gymnastics by Georgina Serrano, Mexico

Volleyball, by Maria de Jesus Hernandez, Mexico

The students come from four countries - Honduras, Mexico, Russia, and Ukraine.

Can you draw their countries on the map?

5: ENROLLING IN SCHOOL

LOOK AT THE PHOTO: Think about your first day in school.
Circle all the words which describe your feelings on your first day in school.

1. happy   unhappy
2. comfortable   uncomfortable
3. scared   not scared
4. confused   not confused
5. excited   not excited

TAKE TURN WITH A PARTNER: Describe your first day in school.

Example: "On the first day of school, I was _____."

Ask your partner these questions:

1. Why are you studying English?
2. What was your first day in this class?
3. Who was your first friend in this class?
4. What do you like about this class?
5. What don't you like about this class?

LINE-UP 1: Ask your classmates: "How long have you studied English?"
Form a line. The person who has studied English the longest begins the line. Continue forming the line. The person who has studied English the shortest time stands at the other end.

LINE-UP 2: Ask your classmates: "How long have you lived in the U.S.?"
Form a line. The person who has lived here the longest begins the line.

Let's read a student's story about enrolling in school.

My First Day
by **Zoila Chagoya**
Venice Adult School

In January 1993, seven years after I arrived in Los Angeles, I decided to learn English. My friends told me that I needed to go to this school. I only knew these words: "Good morning," "Hi," and "Thank you." I was very embarrassed because I didn't know what I was saying.

When I came to the office, two other people were in line. I asked them, "Is this line to enroll in school?" I asked in Spanish, of course, and they answered, "Yes." I stood in line for about five minutes. I was nervous and thought about how to say, "I want to learn English." In the office there was a person who spoke Spanish and I was comfortable. I enrolled in Level One.

At that time I didn't understand any English. Now, after sixteen months I'm very happy and thankful for my class and my teacher. Now, I can understand and speak English.

Share with a partner: What do you like about Zoila's story?

CHECK YOUR UNDERSTANDING: Talk about these questions with your class. Then write your answers.

1. What is Zoila's native language? _____

2. When did Zoila enroll in school to learn English? _____

3. What English words did she know before she enrolled in school? _____

_____

4. How did Zoila feel when she spoke the words? _____

5. How is her English now? _____

WRITE A STORY: Talk about these questions with a partner. Then write your answers.

1. What is your native language? _____

2. When did you enroll in school to learn English? _____

3. What English words did you know before you enrolled in school? _____

_____

4. How did you feel when you enrolled in school? _____

5. How is your English now?

Write a story about enrolling in school to learn English.

Learning English

_____

_____

_____

_____

_____

Read your story to a partner.
Then your partner can share something she or he liked about your story.

6: MY SCHOOL

BRAINSTORM WITH A GROUP: Think about your school and make a list of words.

Examples: buildings, tables, desks

_____   _____   _____

_____   _____   _____

_____   _____   _____

DRAW A PICTURE OF YOUR CLASSROOM.

Read the sentences. Circle True or False. Then check your answers with the class.

1. My classroom is large.	True	False
2. My teacher is a man.	True	False
3. My classroom has pictures on the walls.	True	False
4. My class begins at 8:30 AM.	True	False
5. There are a lot of books in my classroom.	True	False
6. There are 30 students in my class today.	True	False

Let's read a student's story about her school.

My School

by **Luisa Ochoa**

South Gate Adult School

My school's name is South Gate Adult Learning Center. It is on the corner of State Street and Missouri Street. It is a big school. It has many rooms and a parking lot for the students.

My classroom is big. It has beautiful posters, big maps, and a lot of windows. My classmates are nice.

I have two classes every day. I have four hours of classes every day. The first class begins at 8:30 AM. My teacher is Mr. Green. The second class begins at 10:45 AM. My second teacher is a woman. Her name is Mrs. Hughes. We call her Barbara. They are good teachers.

Share with a partner: What do you like about Luisa's story?

CHECK YOUR UNDERSTANDING: Talk about these questions with your class. Then write your answers.

1. What school does Luisa go to? _____

2. Where is her school located? _____

3. What does her classroom look like? _____

_____

4. What are her teachers' names? _____

5. What times are Luisa's classes? _____

WRITE A STORY: Talk about these questions with a partner. Then write your answers.

1. What school do you go to? _____

2. Where is your school located? _____

3. What does your classroom look like? _____

_____

4. What is your English teacher's name? _____

5. What time is your English class? _____

6. What do you like about your class? _____

Write a story about your school.

My School

_____

_____

_____

_____

_____

Read your story to a partner.
Then your partner can share something he or she liked about your story.

7: MY BEST FRIEND

LOOK AT THE PHOTO: Discuss the questions with a partner.

1. Who is your best friend now?
2. Where does your friend live?
3. What do you like about your friend?
4. Where did you meet your friend?
5. What are some things you like to talk about together?
6. What are some things you like to do together?

Circle the words that describe your friend's personality.

serious	funny	quiet	loud
hard-working	lazy	friendly	shy
kind	unkind	happy	unhappy

Other words: _____

_____

_____

Talk to another partner. Describe your friend's personality. Use the words from the list.

Begin with: "My best <u>friend's name</u> is _____.

She (or he) is a (an) _____ person."

Let's read a student's story about his best friend.

My Best Friend
by Cesar Gutierrez
South Gate Adult School

My best friend's name is Alex. He is very funny and he talks a lot. He has black eyes and hair. He is short. He is friendly and talkative, and he has a great smile. We played soccer together every Sunday in Long Beach.

I met Alex in school and we were roommates for three years. Alex works as a truck driver now. He moved to San Francisco with his family. I miss him very much.

Share with a partner: What do you like about Cesar's story?

CHECK YOUR UNDERSTANDING: Talk about these questions with your class.
Then write your answers.

1. Who is Cesar's best friend? _____

2. Where did Cesar meet Alex? _____

3. What did they do together? _____

4. Describe Alex's personality. _____

5. What does Alex look like? _____

WRITE A STORY: Talk about these questions with a partner. Then write your answers.

1. Who is your best friend? _____

2. Where did you meet your friend? _____

3. Describe your friend's personality. _____

4. What does your best friend look like? _____

5. What do you like to do together? _____

_____

Write a story about your best friend.

My Best Friend

_____

_____

_____

_____

_____

_____

Read your story to a partner.
Then your partner can share something she or he liked about your story.

8: HOMEWORK

LOOK AT THE PHOTO: Discuss the questions with your class.

1. What is homework?

2. Do you have homework from your classes?

3. Who helps you with your homework?

4. Do you like doing your homework?

GROUP SURVEY: Work in a group of four. Write the names of the students in your group. Ask the questions below and write the answers.

Do you have homework?

Does anyone help you?

Do you like doing your homework?

Name	Homework?		Help?		Homework?	
	Yes	No	Yes	No	Likes	Doesn't like
Example: *Maria*	X			X	X	

Answer the questions about your group's chart.

1. How many students in your group have homework? _____

2. How many students get help with their homework? _____

3. How many students like doing their homework? _____

4. How many students don't like doing their homework? _____

Let's read a student's story about his homework.

My Homework
by **Vadik Mendelson**
Fairfax High School

When I was between nine and twelve years old, I was in elementary school. I needed to do homework almost every day, but I wanted to go out and play soccer or other games with my friends. My mother didn't permit me to go out until I did my homework.

I solved that problem easily. Sometimes I did my homework, but not correctly. Sometimes I told my mother that I would do my homework after I went out with my friends. Usually my mother believed me.

Share with a partner: What do you like about Vadik's story?

CHECK YOUR UNDERSTANDING: Talk about these questions with your class.
Then write your answers.

1. What did Vadik want to do instead of his homework? _____

2. What did Vadik's mother want him to do? _____

3. Did Vadik do his homework carefully? _____

WRITE A STORY: Think about a class in which you had homework.
Talk about these questions with a partner. Then write your answers.

1. What class was it? _____

2. What kind of homework did you have? _____

3. Who helped you with your homework? _____

4. What did you learn from doing your homework? _____

5. Did you like your homework? Why or why not? _____

_____

Write a story about doing your homework.

My Homework

_____

_____

_____

_____

_____

_____

Read your story to a partner.
Then your partner can share something she or he liked about your story.

9: TESTS

LOOK AT THE PHOTO: Discuss the questions with your class.

1. What is a test?
2. Why do students take tests?
3. How many classes are you taking now?
4. Do you have tests?
5. Do you study for your tests?
6. Are your tests easy or difficult?

GROUP SURVEY: Work in a group of four. Write the names of the students in your group. Ask each student to name one of their classes. Then ask the questions below and write the answers.

Do you have tests?

Do you study for your tests?

Are your tests easy or difficult?

Name	Class	Tests? Yes	No	Study? Yes	No	Tests? Easy	Difficult
Example: *Chong*	*ESL*	X		X			X

TAKE A TURN: Use the information in your group's chart to talk about each person.

Example: Chong has an ESL class. He studies for his tests. The tests are difficult.

Let's read a student's story about taking a test.

The Test
by **Yelena Tovbina**
Fairfax High School

When I was thirteen years old, I told my mom that I didn't want to go to school the next day because there was going to be a big test. I was not ready. I was very nervous. She told me that I was going to school anyway because my reason was not good.

When I woke up the next day, she asked if I was going to school. I said, "Yes," and I made the right decision. I got a "B" on the test and I was happy.

Share with a partner: What do you like about Yelena's story?

CHECK YOUR UNDERSTANDING: Talk about these questions with your class. Then write your answers.

1. Why didn't Yelena want to go to school? _____

2. How did Yelena feel about taking the test? _____

3. What did Yelena's mother do? _____

4. What did Yelena decide to do? _____

5. What grade did Yelena receive on the test? _____

WRITE A STORY: Think about a test you took. Talk about these questions with a partner. Then write your answers.

1. What class was your test in? _____

2. Who helped you study for the test? _____

3. Was the test easy or difficult? _____

4. Did you understand all the questions? _____

5. How did you feel when you took the test? _____

Write a story about taking a test.

A Test

_____

_____

_____

_____

_____

_____

_____

Read your story to a partner.
Then your partner can share something he or she liked about your story.

10: AFTER-SCHOOL ACTIVITIES

LOOK AT THE PHOTO: Discuss the questions with your class.

1. Do you have sports or exercise classes at your school?
2. What are some sports?
3. Are the sports or classes during school or after school?
4. What are some after-school activities?
5. What after-school activities do you like?

Look at the pictures below. Then answer the questions.

1. baseball
2. volleyball
3. gymnastics
4. biking
5. swimming
6. soccer

1. Which sports are team sports?
2. In which sports do the players wear a uniform?
3. What do the players do?

PICTURE RE-TELL: Work with a partner. One partner talks about Pictures 1, 3, and 5. The other partner talks about pictures 2, 4, and 6.

Example: Baseball is a team sport. The players wear uniforms and baseball caps. The batter hits the ball.

Let's read two students' stories about their favorite after-school activities.

My Favorite Sport - Gymnastics
by **Georgina Serrano**
South Gate Adult School

When I was in high school, gymnastics was my favorite sport. My mother made my uniform because it was too expensive to buy. She bought me a pair of shoes in a sporting goods store.

I went to gymnastics three days a week. I finished my regular class at 2:00 PM. After that, I went home and ate lunch. I came back at 3:30 PM. From 3:30 to 6:30 I had gymnastics. After the class finished, we took a cold shower. The first days we yelled because the water was freezing cold.

I loved my gym clothes, my shoes and my friends. I really enjoyed that time. I didn't think that time was special in my life, but now, I do.

Volleyball
by **Maria de Jesus Hernandez**
South Gate Adult School

When I was thirteen years old, I liked to play volleyball in school. Every day when my classes ended, some classmates and I played volleyball.

I loved to play it, but many times my mother asked me, "Why are you coming home late?" I answered, "Because the teacher asked me to clean the classroom."

I didn't want to let my mother know I played volleyball because she didn't want me to play. She told me, "Volleyball is a game for men and not for girls." She wanted me at home to help take care of my brothers.

Share with a partner: What do you like about their stories?

CHECK YOUR UNDERSTANDING: Read the questions and put an X in the correct column. Then check your answers with the class.

Georgina	Maria

1. Who played sports after school?

2. Who practiced gymnastics from 3:30 to 6:30 PM?

3. Who played volleyball everyday?

4. Whose mother made a uniform?

5. Who didn't wear a special uniform?

6. Whose mother said volleyball was a game for men?

7. Who told her mother she cleaned the classroom after school?

Think about a sport or exercise you like to do.
Talk about these questions with a partner. Then write your answers.

1. What is your favorite sport? _____

2. Do you play on a team? _____

3. What are three things you like about your favorite sport? _____

_____

_____

Write a story about playing your favorite sport or doing exercise.

My Favorite Sport or Exercise

_____

_____

_____

_____

_____

_____

Read your story to a partner.
Then your partner can share something he or she liked about your story.

Beginning Stories from the Heart

FIND SOMEONE*: Ask your classmates a question. If your classmate's answer is "Yes," ask your classmate to write his or her name on the line next to the sentence.

1. _____ likes his or her teachers.

2. _____ likes doing homework.

3. _____ studies after school with a friend.

4. _____ feels nervous taking a test.

5. _____ likes to play sports.

GUIDED IMAGE*: Close your eyes and think about your school. Now begin to write.

When I closed my eyes ...

1. I saw _____

2. I heard _____

3. I thought _____

4. I felt _____

THINK ABOUT THE UNIT: Answer the questions. Discuss your answers with a partner.

1. Circle the lesson you think is the most interesting. 5   6   7   8   9   10

   Why do you like it? _____

2. Circle the student's story you like the most.   **My First Day**   **My School**
   My Best Friend   **My Homework**   **The Test**
   My Favorite Sport - Gymnastics   **Volleyball**
   Why do you like it? _____

3. Write the title of your story that you like the best. _____

   Why do you like it? _____

FAVORITE THINGS

INTRODUCTION TO THE UNIT.

This unit has stories from three students. These are the stories:

Stuffed Chicken, by Fidelia Cadenas, Nicaragua

Sandals, by Mario Castellanos, Mexico

Dancing, by Jose Cardozo, Mexico

The students come from two countries - Nicaragua and Mexico.

Can you find their countries on the map?

Beginning Stories from the Heart

11: FAVORITE FOOD

LOOK AT THE PHOTO: The food is for a holiday meal. Think about what you eat for a holiday meal. Write the names of the foods on the lines.

_____

_____

_____

_____

_____

GROUP SURVEY: Work in a group of four. Write the names of the students in your group. Then ask the questions below and write the answers.

What is your favorite food?

When do you eat this food?

What are the most important ingredients?

Name	Favorite Food	When?	Ingredients
Example: David	turkey	Thanksgiving	turkey and bread stuffing

TAKE A TURN: Use the information in your group's chart to talk about each person.

Example: David's favorite food is turkey.

He likes to eat it on Thanksgiving.

The most important ingredients are turkey and the bread stuffing.

Let's read a student's story about her favorite food.

Stuffed Chicken

by **Fidelia Cadenas**

Evans Adult School

In Nicaragua there is special excitement on December 24th. It is a national holiday and the happiest day of the year. At midnight our family and friends have a special dinner and a happy party. The national favorite food is "gallena rellena." This is boneless stuffed chicken. It tastes really good! It is usually cooked at home, but you can buy it at high prices in some restaurants.

It takes patience to make the stuffed chicken. It is a long process. You need many things such as: a hen, some pork, raisins, green olives, capers, mint, green and red peppers, potatoes, tomatoes, onions, garlic, butter and spices.

Everybody loves this food. It is my favorite food because it is nutritious, delicious, and healthy.

Share with a partner: What do you like about Fidelia's story?

Beginning Stories from the Heart

CHECK YOUR UNDERSTANDING: Talk about these questions with your class. Then write your answers.

1. What special food does Fidelia eat at midnight on Dec. 24? _____

_____

2. What ingredients does she use to make it? _____

_____

3. What are the three reasons it is her favorite food? _____

_____

WRITE A STORY: Talk about these questions with a partner. Then write your answers.

1. What is your favorite food? _____

2. When do you like to eat it? _____

3. What ingredients are in your favorite food? _____

_____

4. Who cooks your favorite food? _____

Write a story about your favorite food.

My Favorite Food

_____

_____

_____

_____

_____

Read your story to a partner.
Then your partner can share something she or he liked about your story.

12: FAVORITE CLOTHES

LOOK AT THE PHOTO: This person is wearing her favorite clothes. Think about your favorite clothes. Write the names and colors of your favorite clothes.

Example: blue jeans, yellow dress

_____

_____

_____

_____

_____

Circle all the words which describe the clothing you are wearing today.

solid color	sleeveless	round neck	sandals
checked	long-sleeved	V neck	boots
striped	short-sleeved	turtle neck	tennis shoes
print	roll-up sleeves		work shoes
plaid			dressy shoes

CORNERS: Look at your clothing. Go to Corner 1 if your are wearing jeans. Go to Corner 2 if you are wearing slacks. Go to Corner 3 if you are wearing a skirt. Go to Corner 4 if you are wearing a dress.

TALK TO A PARTNER: Describe your clothing.

Example: I am wearing a print dress.

The dress has a round neck and short sleeves.

I like this dress because it is comfortable.

Let's read a student's story about his first pair of new shoes.

Sandals

by **Mario Castellanos**

South Gate Adult School

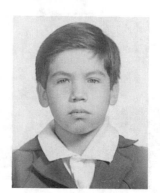

Mario when
he was a boy

My family was very poor. I was ten years old when my mother bought me my first pair of new shoes. I was very, very happy. I showed them to all the people. I put them on to go to church. I felt very good because this was my first pair of new shoes. I remember that I always wore red pants and different kinds of shirts, but the most important thing was my shoes. I always wore them everywhere. I was always happy wearing these clothes.

Share with a partner: What do you like about Mario's story?

CHECK YOUR UNDERSTANDING: Talk about these questions with your class. Then write your answers.

1. Was Mario's family rich or poor? _____

2. When did Mario get his first pair of shoes? _____

3. Who bought the new shoes for Mario? _____

4. Where did he wear the new shoes? _____

5. How did Mario feel when he wore the new shoes? _____

WRITE A STORY: Think about the shoes or clothes you wore as a child. Talk about these questions with a partner. Then write your answers.

1. What were your favorite clothes when you were a child? _____

_____

2. Where did you get them? _____

3. Where did you like to wear them? _____

4. When did you like to wear them? _____

Write a story about your favorite clothes.

My Favorite Clothes

_____

_____

_____

_____

_____

_____

**Read your story to a partner.
Then your partner can share something he or she liked about your story.**

Beginning Stories from the Heart

13: FAVORITE ACTIVITY

BRAINSTORM WITH YOUR CLASS: Say the names of dances and your teacher will write them on the chalkboard. Copy some of the dances you know.

_____	_____	_____
_____	_____	_____
_____	_____	_____
_____	_____	_____

GROUP SURVEY: Work in a group of four. Write the names of the students in your group. Then ask these questions and write the answers.

What's your favorite dance?

Is it fast or slow?

Do you dance alone, with a partner, or in a group?

Do you prefer the dances from your country or the dances in the U.S.?

Name	Favorite dance	Fast	Slow	Alone	With a partner	In a group	From native country	In the U.S.
Example: _Yolanda_	_tango_	X			X		X	

TAKE A TURN: Use the information in your group's chart to talk about each person.

Example: Yolanda likes the tango.

The tango is a fast dance.

She dances the tango with a partner

She prefers the dances from her country.

Let's read a student's story about dancing.

Dancing

by **Jose Cardozo**

South Gate Adult School

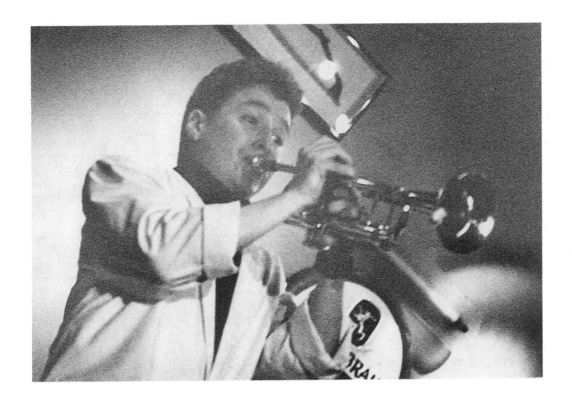

I like to dance because it is very exciting. I remember one time I went dancing with my friend, Alicia. She was a special friend. I invited her to dance with me because she knew how to dance La Quebradita very well. So, I wanted to dance with her because I wanted to see how we danced together. She accepted my invitation. Then she asked her parents. They told her, "OK, you can go." Then we went dancing at a club. I was very happy because we danced well together.

Share with a partner: What do you like about Jose's story?

**CHECK YOUR UNDERSTANDING: Talk about these questions with your class.
Then write your answers.**

1. Who did Jose like to go dancing with? _____

2. Where did they go to dance? _____

3. What dance did Jose do with Alicia? _____

**WRITE A STORY: Think about a dance you like.
Talk about these questions with a partner. Then write your answers.**

1. What is your favorite dance? _____

2. Do you like to dance fast or slow? _____

3. Who do you like to dance with? _____

4. Where do you like to dance? _____

5. Do you like the dances from your country, from the U.S. or both? _____

_____

Write a story about your favorite dance.

My Favorite Dance

_____

_____

_____

_____

_____

_____

_____

**Read your story to a partner.
Then your partner can share something she or he liked about your story.**

END OF UNIT

FIND SOMEONE*: Ask your classmate a question. If your classmate's answer is, "Yes," ask your classmate to write his or her name on the line next to the sentence.

1. _____ is wearing blue jeans.

2. _____ is wearing a T shirt.

3. _____ is wearing a dress.

4. _____ is wearing a watch.

5. _____ is wearing a plaid shirt.

6. _____ likes American food.

7. _____ likes Mexican food.

8. _____ likes Chinese food.

9. _____ likes food from his or her native country.

10. _____ likes to eat fish.

11. _____ likes to eat steak.

12. _____ likes to buy new clothes.

13. _____ likes to wear new clothes on the holidays.

14. _____ likes to wear old clothes most of the time.

15. _____ likes to dance at parties.

16. _____ likes to dance in clubs.

17. _____ likes to dance to American music.

18. _____ likes dances from his or her native country.

19. _____ likes fast dancing.

20. _____ likes slow dancing.

END OF UNIT

**GUIDED IMAGE*: Close your eyes and think about your school.
Now begin to write.**

When I closed my eyes ...

1. I saw _____

_____

_____

2. I heard _____

_____

_____

3. I thought _____

_____

_____

4. I felt _____

_____

THINK ABOUT THE UNIT: Answer the questions. Discuss your answers with a partner.

1. Circle the lesson you think is the most interesting: 11   12   13

   Why do you like it? _____

2. Circle the student's story you like the most: **Stuffed Chicken**
   Sandals   Dancing
   Why do you like it? _____

3. Write the title of your story that you like the best. _____

   Why do you like it? _____

SPECIAL EVENTS

INTRODUCTION TO THE UNIT.
This unit has stories from five students. These are the stories:

Chinese New Year, by Cindy Tse, China

Ethiopian New Year, by Mulugeta Gebrmichael, Ethiopia

Quinceañera, by Trinidad Nuñez, Mexico

Honduran Independence Day, by Marco Martinez, Honduras

Mother's Day, by Flor Galindo, Mexico

The students come from four countries - China, Ethiopia, Mexico, and Honduras.

Can you draw their countries on the map?

14: NEW YEAR'S DAY

LOOK AT THE CALENDAR: Discuss the questions with your class.

S M T W T F S	S M T W T F S	S M T W T F S	S M T W T F S
JANUARY	FEBRUARY	MARCH	APRIL
①2 3 4 5 6	1 2 3	1 2	1 2 3 4 5 6
7 8 9 10 11 12 13	4 5 6 7 8 9 10	3 4 5 6 7 8 9	7 8 9 10 11 12 13
14 15 16 17 18 19 20	11 12 13 14 15 16 17	10 11 12 13 14 15 16	14 15 16 17 18 19 20
21 22 23 24 25 26 27	18 19 20 21 22 23 24	17 18 19 20 21 22 23	21 22 23 24 25 26 27
28 29 30 31	25 26 27 28 29	24 25 26 27 28 29 30	28 29 30
		31	
MAY	JUNE	JULY	AUGUST
1 2 3 4	1	1 2 3 4 5 6	1 2 3
5 6 7 8 9 10 11	2 3 4 5 6 7 8	7 8 9 10 11 12 13	4 5 6 7 8 9 10
12 13 14 15 16 17 18	9 10 11 12 13 14 15	14 15 16 17 18 19 20	11 12 13 14 15 16 17
19 20 21 22 23 24 25	16 17 18 19 20 21 22	21 22 23 24 25 26 27	18 19 20 21 22 23 24
26 27 28 29 30 31	23 24 25 26 27 28 29	28 29 30 31	25 26 27 28 29 30 31
	30		
SEPTEMBER	OCTOBER	NOVEMBER	DECEMBER
1 2 3 4 5 6 7	1 2 3 4 5	1 2	1 2 3 4 5 6 7
8 9 10 11 12 13 14	6 7 8 9 10 11 12	3 4 5 6 7 8 9	8 9 10 11 12 13 14
15 16 17 18 19 20 21	13 14 15 16 17 18 19	10 11 12 13 14 15 16	15 16 17 18 19 20 21
22 23 24 25 26 27 28	20 21 22 23 24 25 26	17 18 19 20 21 22 23	22 23 24 25 26 27 28
29 30	27 28 29 30 31	24 25 26 27 28 29 30	29 30 ㉛

1. When are New Year's Eve and New Year's Day celebrated in your country?

2. What are some things people do on New Year's in your country?

3. When are New Year's Eve and New Year's Day celebrated in the U.S.?

4. What do you like to do on New Year's Eve?

5. What do you like to do on New Year's Day?

GROUP SURVEY: Work in a group of four. Write the names of the students in your group. Ask the questions below about New Year's Eve and write the answers.

Do you like to stay up late?

Do you spend time with your friends or family?

Do you like to eat special food? If so, what is it?

Name	stay up late?	family?	friends?	special food?
Example: *Natalia*	*yes*	*yes*	*yes*	*champagne and cake*

TAKE A TURN: Use the information in your group's chart to talk about each person.

Example: Natalia stays up late on New Year's Eve.

She spends time with her family and friends.

She eats cake and drinks champagne.

Let's read two students' stories about New Years' Day.

Chinese New Year

by **Cindy Tse**

Evans Adult School

We like to celebrate Chinese New Year. This is a big holiday. We usually buy a lot of candy, sweet coconut chestnuts, and cookies to give to our friends and relatives.

On that day every child gets up early in the morning and everyone wears new clothes and new shoes. To everyone we say good things, for example, "Happy New Year!" "Good luck!" "Good health!" and "Make a lot of money!" Parents give their children two red envelopes with some money inside for good luck. Children like to watch fireworks. Most people visit their friends or relatives.

We have special food to celebrate the new year: rice, vegetables, chicken, fish, and roast pork. We cook them with soy sauce, green onions, and mustard sauce.

I like my mother's soup. My mother usually puts in some pork, chicken, mushrooms, dry oysters, and seaweed. She boils it for about two hours and then sprinkles it with a little salt. I like the taste. It is very delicious.

Share with a partner: What do you like about Cindy's story?

Ethiopian New Year
by **Mulugeta Gebrmichael**
Evans Adult School

Ethiopian New Year is the most important holiday of the year for Ethiopian people. We celebrate the new year by cleaning the house. Everyone wears new clothes. Children get New Year's gifts from their families.

On New Year's Day, the food is special. The most famous food is made with hot red pepper, beef or chicken, butter, and a lot of spices. We eat that with "injera" which is a kind of bread.

The family has a big dinner together. They enjoy the special food.

Share with a partner: What do you like about Mulugeta's story?

CHECK YOUR UNDERSTANDING: Read the questions and put an X in the correct column. Then check your answers with the class.

	China	Ethiopia
1. They give cookies and candy to friends at New Year's.		
2. They eat special food on New Year's Day.		
3. They wear new clothes.		
4. They eat "injera."		
5. They eat a special soup.		
6. Children receive red envelopes with money.		
7. Children watch fireworks.		

WRITE A STORY: New Year is usually a time to make plans for the new year. What do you want to do next year? Make a list of the things you want to do. Share your list with a partner.

_____

_____

_____

_____

Write a story about what you want to do next year.

Next Year

_____

_____

_____

_____

_____

Read your story to a partner.
Then your partner can share something she or he liked about your story.

Beginning Stories from the Heart

LOOK AT THE PHOTO: With the class, write the things people like to do on their birthday.

Example: have a birthday cake, get gifts

_____

_____

_____

_____

LINE-UP - Ask your classmates: "When is your birthday?"
Form a line. The person who has the first birthday in the year begins the line.
Continue forming the line according to your birthdays.

Ask the person next to you in line: "How do you want to celebrate your next birthday?"

You can use some of the sentences below in your answers.

I want to eat my favorite foods at a restaurant.

I want to have a party with my family and friends.

I don't want to celebrate it because I am too old.

I want to return to my country.

I don't want to remember this birthday.

I want to go to the movies.

I don't want to do anything special.

I want to go on a vacation.

I want to talk to a good friend.

I want to dance at my favorite club.

Let's read a student's story about an important birthday.

Quinceañera

by **Trinidad Nuñez**

South Gate Adult School

I remember when I was going to be 15 years old. My family gave a party for me. I was in Mexico City on February 19, 1989. I wore a white dress and high heeled shoes. Almost all my family was there. I felt happy and nervous at the same time. Everything was okay. I danced the waltz with my oldest brother. I had two big cakes.

A man made a videotape of the party. The next day I saw the tape. I didn't like it. On the tape I was chewing gum when I danced with a guy. I looked terrible! Since that time I haven't chewed gum again!

Share with a partner: What do you like about Trinidad's story?

CHECK YOUR UNDERSTANDING: Talk about these questions with your class. Then write your answers.

1. How old was Trinidad on Feb. 19, 1989? _____

2. What celebration did her family have for her? _____

3. What did Trinidad wear to the party? _____

4. What did she do at the party? _____

WRITE A STORY: Talk about these questions with a partner. Then write your answers.

1. How old are you? _____

2. Do you remember a birthday party for you or another person? _____

3. Who was at the party? _____

4. What did you do at the party? _____

5. Did anything funny, special, or unusual happen at the party? _____

_____

Write a story about an important birthday celebration.

A Birthday Celebration

_____

_____

_____

_____

_____

_____

Read your story to a partner.
Then your partner can share something he or she liked about your story.

16: INDEPENDENCE DAY

LOOK AT THE CALENDAR: Discuss the questions with your class.

1996

JANUARY	FEBRUARY	MARCH	APRIL
S M T W T F S	S M T W T F S	S M T W T F S	S M T W T F S
1 2 3 4 5 6	1 2 3	1 2	1 2 3 4 5 6
7 8 9 10 11 12 13	4 5 6 7 8 9 10	3 4 5 6 7 8 9	7 8 9 10 11 12 13
14 15 16 17 18 19 20	11 12 13 14 15 16 17	10 11 12 13 14 15 16	14 15 16 17 18 19 20
21 22 23 24 25 26 27	18 19 20 21 22 23 24	17 18 19 20 21 22 23	21 22 23 24 25 26 27
28 29 30 31	25 26 27 28 29	24 25 26 27 28 29 30	28 29 30
		31	

MAY	JUNE	JULY	AUGUST
1 2 3 4	1	1 2 3 4 5 6	1 2 3
5 6 7 8 9 10 11	2 3 4 5 6 7 8	7 8 9 10 11 12 13	4 5 6 7 8 9 10
12 13 14 15 16 17 18	9 10 11 12 13 14 15	14 15 16 17 18 19 20	11 12 13 14 15 16 17
19 20 21 22 23 24 25	16 17 18 19 20 21 22	21 22 23 24 25 26 27	18 19 20 21 22 23 24
26 27 28 29 30 31	23 24 25 26 27 28 29	28 29 30 31	25 26 27 28 29 30 31
	30		

SEPTEMBER	OCTOBER	NOVEMBER	DECEMBER
1 2 3 4 5 6 7	1 2 3 4 5	1 2	1 2 3 4 5 6 7
8 9 10 11 12 13 14	6 7 8 9 10 11 12	3 4 5 6 7 8 9	8 9 10 11 12 13 14
15 16 17 18 19 20 21	13 14 15 16 17 18 19	10 11 12 13 14 15 16	15 16 17 18 19 20 21
22 23 24 25 26 27 28	20 21 22 23 24 25 26	17 18 19 20 21 22 23	22 23 24 25 26 27 28
29 30	27 28 29 30 31	24 25 26 27 28 29 30	29 30 31

1. What is Independence Day?

2. What date is Independence Day in the U.S.?

3. What country did the U.S. get their independence from?

4. When was the American Revolution?

5. What are some things people do on July 4th in the U.S.?

6. Do you celebrate July 4th? What do you do?

BRAINSTORM IN A GROUP OF FOUR: Make a list of all the things you like to do on your country's Independence Day or on July 4th.

_____

_____

_____

_____

_____

_____

_____

Write your group's list on the chalkboard.

Compare your group's list with the other groups' lists. Copy any new words in your book.

Let's read a student's story about a national holiday.

Beginning Stories from the Heart

Honduran Independence Day
by **Marco Martinez**
Los Angeles High School

Independence Day is an important day in my country, Honduras, because it is the day we declared our independence from Spain. On September 15, 1821, General Francisco Morazan and his soldiers defeated the Spanish army. He declared all Central America free and independent countries.

Independence Day is a nice day in my country because people go out in the street to see the soldiers and college students. They march and play music with drums, flutes, and trumpets to celebrate Independence Day.

When I lived in my country, I used to play music on Independence Day with my band. Now, I just remember how it was. We used to go to parties and laugh with our friends. There was nothing to worry about. When night came, I had a big dinner with my family.

Share with a partner: What do you like about Marco's story?

CHECK YOUR UNDERSTANDING: Talk about these questions with your class.
Then write your answers.

1. What country is Marco from? _____

2. What day is Independence Day in Honduras? _____

3. What do people in Honduras do on Independence Day? _____

_____

4. How did Marco celebrate Independence Day in Honduras? _____

_____

WRITE A STORY: Talk about these questions with a partner. Then write your answers.

1. What country are you from? _____

2. What day is Independence Day or National Day in your country? _____

3. What country did your country get its independence from? _____

4. How is Independence Day or National Day celebrated in your country? _____

_____

Write a story about Independence Day in your country or in the U.S.

Independence Day

_____

_____

_____

_____

_____

Read your story to a partner.
Then your partner can share something he or she liked about your story.

Beginning Stories from the Heart

17: MOTHER'S DAY OR FATHER'S DAY

LOOK AT THE CALENDAR: Discuss the questions with your class.

```
                        1996
  S M T W T F S    S M T W T F S    S M T W T F S    S M T W T F S
  JANUARY          FEBRUARY         MARCH            APRIL
      1 2 3 4 5 6           1 2 3                1 2    1 2 3 4 5 6
  7 8 9 10 11 12 13  4 5 6 7 8 9 10  3 4 5 6 7 8 9    7 8 9 10 11 12 13
  14 15 16 17 18 19 20  11 12 13 14 15 16 17  10 11 12 13 14 15 16  14 15 16 17 18 19 20
  21 22 23 24 25 26 27  18 19 20 21 22 23 24  17 18 19 20 21 22 23  21 22 23 24 25 26 27
  28 29 30 31      25 26 27 28 29     24 25 26 27 28 29 30  28 29 30
                                     31

  MAY              JUNE             JULY             AUGUST
        1 2 3 4                  1   1 2 3 4 5 6          1 2 3
  5 6 7 8 9 10 11  2 3 4 5 6 7 8   7 8 9 10 11 12 13  4 5 6 7 8 9 10
  12 13 14 15 16 17 18  9 10 11 12 13 14 15  14 15 16 17 18 19 20  11 12 13 14 15 16 17
  19 20 21 22 23 24 25  16 17 18 19 20 21 22  21 22 23 24 25 26 27  18 19 20 21 22 23 24
  26 27 28 29 30 31  23 24 25 26 27 28 29  28 29 30 31      25 26 27 28 29 30 31
                   30

  SEPTEMBER        OCTOBER          NOVEMBER         DECEMBER
  1 2 3 4 5 6 7        1 2 3 4 5            1 2   1 2 3 4 5 6 7
  8 9 10 11 12 13 14  6 7 8 9 10 11 12  3 4 5 6 7 8 9   8 9 10 11 12 13 14
  15 16 17 18 19 20 21  13 14 15 16 17 18 19  10 11 12 13 14 15 16  15 16 17 18 19 20 21
  22 23 24 25 26 27 28  20 21 22 23 24 25 26  17 18 19 20 21 22 23  22 23 24 25 26 27 28
  29 30            27 28 29 30 31   24 25 26 27 28 29 30  29 30 31
```

1. Is there a special day to celebrate mothers in your country?

   When is it?

2. Is there a special day to celebrate fathers in your country?

   When is it?

3. What is something special you like to do on Mother's Day or Father's Day?

4. Who is a special man or woman you like to remember on those days?

MAKE A LIST: Write the things you liked about your mother or another woman who was special to you.

Make another list of the things you liked in your father or another man who was special to you.

Mother	Father
_____	_____
_____	_____
_____	_____
_____	_____
_____	_____
_____	_____

Let's read a student's story about Mother's Day in her country.

Mother's Day

by **Flor Galindo**

Los Angeles High School

In my country, Mexico, we celebrate Mother's Day on May 10th, but in other countries it may be celebrated on a different day.

Each year my family gets together to celebrate this marvelous day. It is very important because we celebrate the person who gave us life. The first thing we do that morning is sing, "Las Manaitas". After the song, we say, "Happy Mother's Day" and give our mother a hug. During the day we make special food in her honor. We give her some flowers and some gifts. My mother enjoys all these things and she makes us feel happy.

Mother's Day is a tradition that lots of people have celebrated for many years.

Share with a partner: What do you like about Flor's story?

CHECK YOUR UNDERSTANDING: Talk about these questions with your class.
Then write your answers.

1. What day is Mother's Day in Mexico? _____

2. Why is Mother's Day is celebrated? _____

_____

3. What are three things Mexican people do for their mothers on Mother's Day?

_____

_____

WRITE A STORY: Talk about these questions with a partner. Then write your answers.

1. Do you celebrate Mother's Day or Father's Day? _____

2. What do you do? _____

_____

Write a story about how you celebrate Mother's Day or Father's Day.

_____ 's Day

_____

_____

_____

_____

_____

_____

Read your story to a partner.
Then your partner can share something he or she liked about your story.

FIND SOMEONE*: Ask your classmate a question. If your classmate's answer is "Yes," ask your classmate to write his or her name on the line next to the sentence.

1. _____ celebrates New Year's Eve on Dec. 31.

2. _____ celebrates New Year's Day on Jan. 1.

3. _____ celebrates more than one New Year's Day in a year.

4. _____ stayed up late on New Year's Eve last year.

5. _____ cooked special food on New Year's Day this year.

6. _____ wore new clothes on New Year's Day this year.

7. _____ received a gift on New Year's Day this year.

8. _____ went to a birthday celebration this year.

9. _____ danced at a celebration this year.

10. _____ wore beautiful clothes at a party this year.

11. _____ celebrated the last July 4th.

12. _____ felt happy on the last July 4th.

13. _____ celebrated their native country's Independence Day.

14. _____ played an instrument on a holiday.

15. _____ sang a special song on a holiday.

16. _____ ate a big holiday dinner with family and friends.

17. _____ celebrated Mother's Day or Father's Day last year.

18. _____ visited his or her family this month.

19. _____ ate special food in a restaurant last month.

GUIDED IMAGE*: Close your eyes and think about your neighborhood. Now begin to write.

When I closed my eyes:

1. I saw _____

_____

2. I heard _____

_____

3. I talked to _____

_____

4. I felt _____

_____

THINK ABOUT THE UNIT: Answer the questions. Discuss your answers with a partner.

1. Circle the lesson you think is the most interesting.   14   15   16   17

Why do you like it? _____

2. Circle the student's story you like the most:

Chinese New Year   **Ethiopian New Year**   **Quinceañera**
Honduran Independence Day   **Mother's Day**

Why do you like it? _____

3. Write the title of your story that you like the best. _____

Why do you like it? _____

FIRST COUNTRY/SECOND COUNTRY

INTRODUCTION TO THE UNIT.

This unit has stories from four students. These are the stories:

Life in Cuba, by **Luis Felipe Morgan**, Cuba

Deciding to Leave El Salvador, by Norma Irene Mendoza, El Salvador

Coming to the United States, by Nada Chambers, Yugoslavia

My First Day in the United States, by My Duyen Thi Nguyen, Vietnam

The students come from four countries - Cuba, El Salvador, Yugoslavia, and Vietnam.

Can you draw their countries on the map?

18: LIFE IN MY COUNTRY

MAKE A LIST: With your class, write the reasons for leaving your native country.
Examples: crime, no jobs

_____

_____

_____

_____

From your list, write the main reason you left your country. _____

_____

Tell a partner about your reason for leaving your native country.

Example: I left because <u>there was a war.</u>

DRAW A PICTURE: Draw something you remember from your home country.

Write a few sentences about your picture.
Show your picture to a partner and read your sentences.

_____

_____

_____

Let's read a student's story about life in his country.

Life in Cuba
by **Luis Felipe Morgan**
Abram Friedman Occupational Center

In Cuba you get up, take a shower in cold water, and walk to the bus stop. You arrive at the bus stop at about 7:00 and wait for the bus. Your job begins at 8:00. You wait and wait and wait at the bus stop. Eight o'clock comes and there's no bus. Nine o'clock comes and there's no bus. Ten o'clock comes and there's no bus. Finally, a bus comes at 11:00, but it's full so it doesn't stop. You give up and go home.

So, in Cuba everybody walks a lot. Shoes cost a lot of money. My brother sold his bicycle to buy a pair of shoes. I am very happy to be in the United States. I don't have to wait for a bus anymore. I have a car. And I have seven pairs of shoes!

Share with a partner: What do you like about Luis' story?

Beginning Stories from the Heart

**CHECK YOUR UNDERSTANDING: Talk about these questions with your class.
Then write your answers.**

1. What did Luis do everyday in Cuba? _____

_____

2. What time did Luis' job begin? _____

3. Why do you think it was difficult to catch a bus in Cuba? _____

_____

4. Are shoes expensive or cheap in Cuba? _____

**WRITE A STORY: Think about your life in your home country.
Answer these questions with a partner. Then write your answers.**

1. What was one big problem you or your family had everyday in your country?

_____

2. What did you or your family try to do to change the problem and make things
    better?

_____

3. What happened? _____

Write a story about a problem in your home country.

A Problem In My Home Country

_____

_____

_____

_____

_____

**Read your story to a partner.
Then your partner can share something he or she liked about your story.**

19: DECIDING TO LEAVE MY COUNTRY

BRAINSTORM WITH YOUR CLASS: Think about all the things you liked about your home country.

Examples: food, holidays, weather

_____

_____

_____

_____

_____

_____

_____

From your list, write the one thing you liked the best about your country. _____

_____

Tell a partner about the thing you liked the best.

STAND UP AND SHARE: Everyone in the class stands up. Your teacher asks one student to answer this question: "What is the one thing you liked best about your country?"

After the student gives his or her opinion, he or she sits down and the other students who agree sit down. Then another student gives an opinion and those who agree sit down.

Let's read a student's story about her decision to leave her country.

Deciding to Leave El Salvador
by Norma Irene Mendoza
Fairfax High School

When I was ten years old, my mother decided to live in Los Angeles. I didn't want to come to Los Angeles because I didn't want to leave my friends and my grandparents. I felt very sad. The conflict was that I had to decide to come to Los Angeles or stay with my grandparents.

My grandparents said that a daughter must be with her mother. I felt bad because it was a big decision and I still loved my grandparents. I decided to come with my mother because I loved her and it was the best thing for me to do.

Share with a partner: What do you like about Norma's story?

CHECK YOUR UNDERSTANDING: Talk about these questions with your class.
Then write your answers.

1. Why did Norma leave El Salvador and come to the U.S.? _____

_____

2. Who didn't Norma want to say good-bye to in El Salvador? _____

3. How old was Norma when her mother came to the U.S.? _____

4. How did Norma feel about her decision to come to the U.S.? _____

_____

WRITE A STORY: Talk about these questions with a partner. Then write your answers.

1. Why did you come to the U.S.? _____

_____

2. How old were you when you came to the U.S.? _____

3. How did you feel after you came here? _____

Write a story about your decision to come to the United States.

Why I Came To The United States

_____

_____

_____

_____

_____

_____

_____

Read your story to a partner.
Then your partner can share something he or she liked about your story.

20: MY TRIP TO THE UNITED STATES

DRAW A MAP: Draw your route to the United States on the map.

1. Draw your native country on the map.

2. Make another X on any places you stopped on the way to the U.S.

3. Make an X on the city you live in now.

4. Draw a line from your country to the city you live in now.

Talk with a partner about these questions.

1. What country were you born in?

2. On what continent is your country?

3. What is the first city you came to in the U.S.?

4. What city do you live in now?

Talk with another partner. Retell your story. Use the map when you explain your story.

Let's read a student's story about her trip to the United States.

Coming to the United States
by **Nada Chambers**
Gardena Adult School

I was born in Yugoslavia. In May of last year I had an American immigration visa in my hands. In June I had to go to the U.S., but I didn't know any English!

First, I went by bus to Budapest. Then I flew to Amsterdam. At the Amsterdam airport, I had to pass a customs inspection before I got on a plane to Minneapolis. The customs officers asked me many questions in English, but I was not able to answer them. When they realized I could speak French, they told me to sit and wait. We waited for some passengers who could speak French. The time between the two flights was short - about one hour. I still waited. I thought I would miss my flight to America. Finally, two French men came. They helped me answer the customs officers. I was thankful to these people.

Share with a partner: What do you like about Nada's story?

CHECK YOUR UNDERSTANDING: Talk about these questions with your class. Then write your answers.

1. Where was Nada born? _____

2. What countries did she pass through on her way to the U.S.? _____

_____

3. What problem did she have with the customs officers? _____

4. Who helped her communicate with the customs officers? _____

WRITE A STORY: Talk about these questions with a partner. Then write your answers.

1. Where were you born? _____

2. What countries did you pass through when you came to the U.S.? _____

_____

3. What was the first big city you came to in the U.S.? _____

4. Where do you live now? _____

Write a story about coming to the United States.

Coming to the United States

_____

_____

_____

_____

_____

_____

_____

Read your story to a partner.
Then your partner can share something he or she liked about your story.

21: FIRST IMPRESSIONS OF THE UNITED STATES

BRAINSTORM WITH YOUR CLASS: Think about your arrival in the U.S. Make a list of words which describe what you saw or how you felt.

Examples: many people, big buildings, afraid, excited

_____

_____

_____

_____

DRAW A PICTURE: What did you see on your first day in the United States?

Write a few sentences about your picture.

Show your picture to a partner and read your sentences.

_____

_____

_____

Let's read a student's story about her first day in the U.S.

My First Day in the United States
by My Duyen Thi Nguyen
Abram Friedman Occupational Center

The first day I arrived in the United States, several things surprised me. First of all, I was surprised to see how big American people are. There were many, many cars on the street, and that surprised me, too. On the way from the airport to my house, I didn't see as many tall buildings as I expected. I saw a few people riding bicycles. I liked that very much. It reminded me of my country, Vietnam.

Share with a partner: What do you like about My Duyen's story?

CHECK YOUR UNDERSTANDING: Talk about these questions with your class. Then write your answers.

1. Where is My Duyen from? _____

2. What are two things which surprised My Duyen on her first day in the U.S.? ____

_____

3. What did she see that made her remember her country? _____

_____

WRITE A STORY: Think about your first year in the United States. Talk about these questions with a partner. Then write your answers.

1. Where did you live when you came to the U.S. ?_____

2. What did you do everyday when you first came to the U.S.? _____

_____

3. Did anything surprise you when you first arrived in the U.S.? _____

What surprised you? _____

_____

Write a story about your first year in the United States.

My First Year in the United States

_____

_____

_____

_____

_____

_____

Read your story to a partner.
Then your partner can share something she or he liked about your story.

FIND SOMEONE*: Ask your classmate a question. If your classmate's answer is "Yes," ask your classmate to write his or her name on the line next to the sentence.

1. _____ lived in a big city in their native country.

2. _____ came from Asia.

3. _____ came from Central or South America.

4. _____ arrived in the U.S. more than two years ago.

5. _____ wants to visit his or her native country next year.

GUIDED IMAGE*: Close your eyes and think about your native country and the United States. Now begin to write.

When I closed my eyes:

In my country _____

_____

In the United States _____

_____

THINK ABOUT THE UNIT: Answer the questions. Discuss your answers with a partner.

1. Circle the lesson you think is the most interesting: 18   19   20   21

   Why do you like it? _____

2. Circle the student's story you like the most:

   Life in Cuba   **Deciding to Leave El Salvador**

   Coming to the U.S.   **My First Day in the U.S.**

   Why do you like it? _____

3. Write the title of your story that you like the best. _____

   Why do you like it? _____

DECISIONS

INTRODUCTION TO THE UNIT.

This unit has stories from five students. These are the stories:

The Car, by Gennady Daych, Russia

Death of My Friend, by Hyung Min Jeon, South Korea

My Father's Advice, by Young J. Lee, South Korea

When My Brother Ran Away, by Hwa Jin Oh, South Korea

My Problem, by Martina Banda, Mexico

The students come from three countries - Russia, South Korea, and Mexico.
Can you draw their countries on the map?

22: FAMILY RULES

LOOK AT THE PHOTO: Discuss the questions with your class.

1. Is there a car in your family?

2. Who can drive the car?

3. Do you know how to drive the car?

4. Are you allowed to drive the car?

5. Where do you go when you drive the car?

BRAINSTORM IN A GROUP OF FOUR: Make a list of the rules in your family.

Example: Always lock the front door to our home.

Come home before midnight.

_____

_____

_____

_____

_____

_____

In your group, decide which category each rule goes into.

The categories are: Safety, Health, Work, School, and Money.

Write the name of each category after the rule.

Example: Always lock the door to our home. (safety)

Let's read a student's story about borrowing his father's car and breaking a family rule.

The Car
by **Gennady Daych**
Fairfax High School

Two months ago, I asked my father to give me his car. I wanted to drive with my friends. He said, "Yes." Then my father said that I had to be home on time.

I had a good time with my friends, but I didn't come home on time. My father was very angry and sad. He yelled at me and said that I'd never get to use his car again. We had a big argument. I didn't talk to my father for one week. Of course, I felt very unhappy.

Share with a partner: What do you like about Gennady's story?

CHECK YOUR UNDERSTANDING: Talk about these questions with your class.
Then write your answers.

1. What did Gennady ask his father? _____

2. What did Mr. Daych tell his son? _____

3. Did Gennady come home on time? _____

4. What did Mr. Daych do? _____

5. How did Gennady feel afterwards? _____

WRITE A STORY: Think about a time you or another family member broke a family rule.
Talk about these questions with a partner. Then write your answers.

1. What was the rule? _____

2. How did you break it? _____

3. What happened? _____

4. How did you feel afterwards? _____

Write a story about breaking a family rule.

Breaking A Family Rule

_____

_____

_____

_____

_____

_____

_____

Read your story to a partner.
Then your partner can share something she or he liked about your story.

23: LOSING SOMEONE

LOOK AT THE PHOTO: Talk about these questions with the class.

1. Do you have a special person who you don't see anymore?

2. What was his or her name?

3. When did you see the special person the last time?

4. How do you feel when you think about them?

5. What are some special things you remember about the person?

Write the name of the person you remember: _____

Circle all the reasons you do not see this person anymore.

1. We stopped seeing each other.

2. I moved to a different place.

3. The person moved to a different place.

4. I left my country.

5. The person left our country.

6. We had an argument.

7. The person died.

8. We are too busy to see each other.

9. We go to different schools.

Let's read a student's story about the loss of a friend.

Death of My Friend

by **Hyung Min Jeon**

Fairfax High School

When I was thirteen years old, my friend died in a car accident. He was my best friend. He lived with his parents, his younger sister and older brother.

His family was very sad and cried. He had the same class with me. He was very kind, so my classmates were also very sad. My teacher cried, too.

I felt very sorrowful. I lost my best friend and I couldn't cope. My mother helped me. My mother said, "Can you try to forget your sadness? I am sad, too, but he is dead. I don't want you to be unable to do anything." So, I decided to try to forget my friend, but sometimes I remember him, Hyun Sik.

Share with a partner: What do you like about Hyung Min's story?

CHECK YOUR UNDERSTANDING: Talk about these questions with your class.
Then write your answers.

1. Who died? _____

2. How did Hyun Sik die? _____

3. How did Hyung Min feel after his friend died? _____

4. What advice did his mother give him? _____

5. Does Hyung Min still remember his friend? _____

WRITE A STORY: Think about someone you do not see anymore. Talk about these questions with a partner. Then write your answers.

1. What is this person's name? _____

2. Was this person a friend or a relative? _____

3. What do you remember about this person? _____

_____

Write a story about a special person you do not see anymore.

A Special Person

_____

_____

_____

_____

_____

_____

_____

Read your story to a partner.
Then your partner can share something he or she liked about your story.

Beginning Stories from the Heart

24: GETTING ADVICE

LOOK AT THE PHOTO: Discuss the questions with your class.

1. Why do people smoke?
2. Is smoking allowed at your school?
3. Where are some places that smoking is not allowed?
4. How can smoking affect a person's health?

Think about your classmates' answers to the first question. Select the main reason why you think people smoke. Write the reason below.

_____

STAND UP AND SHARE: Everyone in the class stands up. Your teacher asks one student to answer this question:

"What do you think are the main reasons people smoke?"

After the student gives his or her opinion, the student sits down and the other students who agree sit down also.

Then another student gives his or her opinion and those students who agree sit down.

GIVE YOUR OPINION: Do you agree or disagree with the following ideas? Circle your answer. Then explain your opinions to a partner.

1. Smoking is OK for adults.	Agree	Disagree
2. Smoking is OK for teens.	Agree	Disagree
3. Smoking should be allowed in restaurants.	Agree	Disagree
4. Smoking should be allowed in schools.	Agree	Disagree
5. Smoking should be allowed in stores.	Agree	Disagree
6. Smoking should be allowed in hospitals.	Agree	Disagree

Let's read a student's story about getting advice.

My Father's Advice
by **Young J. Lee**
Fairfax High School

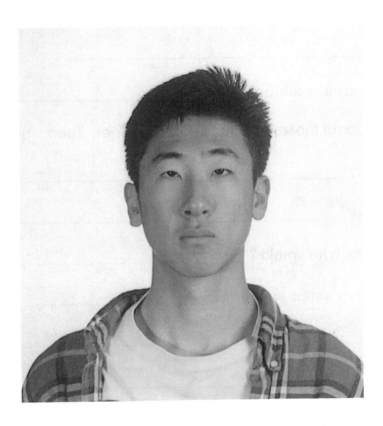

When I was thirteen years old, I had a big problem. It made me very unhappy and I needed help.

I told my father that I smoked. He told me a story. When he was young, he liked to smoke. He didn't know smoking was bad. One day my grandfather saw my father smoking. My grandfather told my father, "Smoking is very bad for your health." My father thought about it. He decided to quit smoking.

I listened to my father's story and his advice. Now, I don't smoke.

Share with a partner: What do you like about Young J.'s story?

CHECK YOUR UNDERSTANDING: Talk about these questions with your class. Then write your answers.

1. What was Young J.'s problem? _____

2. How old was Young J. when he had the problem? _____

3. What did Young J.'s father tell him about the problem? _____

_____

4. Why did Young J. stop smoking? _____

WRITE A STORY: Talk about these questions with a partner. Then write your answers.

1. Do you smoke now? _____

2. Did you ever smoke? _____

3. Do you have friends who smoke? _____

4. What is your opinion about smoking? _____

_____

_____

Write a story about smoking.

Smoking

_____

_____

_____

_____

_____

_____

_____

Read your story to a partner.
Then your partner can share something he or she liked about your story.

25: A FAMILY PROBLEM

BRAINSTORM WITH YOUR CLASS: Make a list of things teens like to do in their free time.

Example: go to movies, dance, play sports

_____

_____

_____

_____

_____

_____

GIVE YOUR OPINION: Work in a group of four. **Discuss this statement.**

There are many problems for teens in the U.S. Some problems are drinking, smoking, drugs, gangs, and violence.

Explain why some teens have these problems. Each person has two minutes to talk.

GIVE YOUR OPINION: Do you agree or disagree with the following ideas? Circle your answer. Then explain your opinions to a partner.

1. Teens need to study more.	Agree	Disagree
2. Teens need to go out, dance, and have a good time.	Agree	Disagree
3. Teens need to spend more time with their families.	Agree	Disagree
4. Teens need to have a lot of rules.	Agree	Disagree
5. Teens need to have more freedom.	Agree	Disagree

Let's read a student's story about a problem in her family.

When My Brother Ran Away
by **Hwa Jin Oh**
Fairfax High School

When I was fourteen years old, I had a big problem. My parents were very busy. They went to work early and came home late. On Sundays they went to meetings or parties. My brother and I had too much free time. My brother had bad friends and got low grades in school. He started to smoke and drink. My parents didn't know, but I knew.

One day he ran away with his friends. For a week he didn't go to school and he didn't come home. I was very sad and my parents were, too. We were very worried. My father looked for him.

A few days later, we found him. My parents gave him a long lecture. My brother realized that it was bad to run away. I was very happy.

When my brother ran away, I also wanted to run away. But I didn't. After the incident, my parents were concerned for us. We tried to be closer than before. We became a good family.

Share with a partner: What do you like about Hwa Jin's story?

CHECK YOUR UNDERSTANDING: Talk about these questions with your class.
Then write your answers.

1. Where were Hwa Jin's parents every day? _____

2. Where were her parents on Sundays? _____

3. What did her brother do in his free time? _____

_____

4. After her brother ran away, how did Hwa Jin and her parents feel? _____

_____

5. Why did her brother come home? _____

WRITE A STORY: Think about a teenager who has a problem. Talk about these questions
with a partner. Then write your answers.

1. What is this person's problem? _____

2. What do you think is the reason for the problem? _____

_____

3. Are there friends or family who can help to solve the problem? _____

4. What other things can be done to solve the problem? _____

_____

Write a story about a teen who has a problem in the U.S.

A Problem

_____

_____

_____

_____

_____

Read your story to a partner.
Then your partner can share something she or he liked about your story.

26: A PROBLEM

TALK WITH A PARTNER: Discuss these questions.

1. What are three things you have to do every day?

2. What are some things you want to do but you don't have time for?

3. How do you feel when you can't do everything you want to do?

4. What are some things you try to do on weekends to catch up?

5. What do you do to rest and relax?

LINE - UP 1 - Ask your classmates: "What time did you go to bed last night?"
Form a line beginning with the earliest time and ending with the latest time.

LINE - UP 2 - Ask your classmates: "What time did you get up this morning?"
Form a line beginning with the earliest time and ending with the latest time.

LINE - UP 3 - Ask your classmates: "How many hours did you sleep last night?"
Form a line beginning with the person who had the most sleep.

Ask the person next to you in line: "What are some things you want to do but don't have enough time to do?"

You can use the words below to begin your answers.

I want to _____, but I can't because _____.

I want to _____, and usually I can.

Let's read a student's story about problems she has with her time.

My Problem
by **Martina Banda**
Gardena Adult School

Right now I have a problem with my daughter. I want to help her with her homework every day, but I don't have enough time. I have to work. I return from work at 5:00 PM. I have to cook, eat, and get ready to go to school. Anyway, I try to help her.

Sometimes, she says, "Mommy, please don't go to school. I want to play with you." I feel bad, but I know and she knows, too, that I have to improve my English to keep helping her with her homework.

Share with a partner: What do you like about Martina's story?

CHECK YOUR UNDERSTANDING: Talk about these questions with your class. Then write your answers.

1. What does Martina have to do when she comes home? _____

_____

2. When does Martina's daughter want her to do? _____

3. Why does Martina study English? _____

4. How do you think Martina feels about this family problem? _____

WRITE A STORY: Talk about these questions with a partner. Then write your answers.

1. What time do you get home? _____

2. What do you have to do when you get home? _____

_____

3. Do you finish everything you have to do? _____

4. How do you feel when you have too much to do? _____

5. What would do you do if you had more time? _____

_____

Write a story about what you have to do at home.

What I Have to do At Home

_____

_____

_____

_____

_____

Read your story to a partner.
Then your partner can share something he or she liked about your story.

FIND SOMEONE*: Ask your classmate a question. If your classmate's answer is "Yes," ask your classmate to write his or her name on the line next to the sentence.

1. _____ has to clean house today.

2. _____ has to study after school today.

3. _____ has to go shopping today.

4. _____ plays sports after school today.

5. _____ has to take care of young children after school.

6. _____ has to work today.

GUIDED IMAGE*: Close your eyes and think about a problem. Now begin to write.

When I closed my eyes:

1. My problem is _____

_____

2. My solution is _____

_____

THINK ABOUT THE UNIT: Answer the questions. Discuss your answers with a partner.

1. Circle the lesson you think is the most interesting. 22   23   24   25   26

    Why do you like it? _____

2. Circle the student's story you liked the most: **The Car   Death of My Friend**
    My Father's Advice   When My Brother Ran Away   My Problem
    Why did you like it? _____

3. Write the title of your story that you like the best. _____

    Why do you like it? _____